WRITE THIS WAY

WRITING FANTASTIC FICTION

JENNIFER JOLINE ANDERSON

DUE	

LERNER PUBLICATIONS ◆ MINNEAPOLIS

Lerner Publications Company
A division of Lerner Publishing Group, Inc.
241 First Avenue North
Minneapolis, MN 55401 USA

For reading levels and more information, look up this title at www.lernerbooks.com.

Main body text set in Dante MT Std 12/15. Typeface provided by Monotype.

Library of Congress Cataloging-in-Publication Data

Anderson, Jennifer Joline.
    Writing fantastic fiction / by Jennifer Joline Anderson.
        pages cm. — (Write this way)
    Includes bibliographical references and index.
    ISBN 978-1-4677-7908-1 (lb : alk. paper) — ISBN 978-1-4677-8290-6 (pb : alk.
paper) — ISBN 978-1-4677-8291-3 (eb pdf)
    1. Fiction—Authorship—Juvenile literature. 2. Creative writing—Juvenile
literature. I. Title.
PN3355.A68 2015
808.3—dc23   2014044105

Manufactured in the United States of America
1 – VP – 7/15/15

Table of Contents

INTRODUCTION

How do you write fantastic fiction? Chances are you're familiar with some of the basic ingredients: interesting characters, a vivid setting, and a gripping plot. To create an original story, you can mix up these ingredients in an endless variety of ways. *Fiction* **refers to stories that are made up, or not true. That means the who, what, when, where, why, and how of a story are up to you, the writer.**

Characters in a work of fiction are often people. But your story's characters could also be animals, as with E. B. White's *Charlotte's Web*. Gods and monsters populate Rick Riordan's *Percy Jackson and the Olympians*, while a woman with supernatural gifts stars in Octavia E. Butler's *Parable of the Sower*. Whatever your characters are like, your job as a fiction writer is to make them real and believable.

The setting of your story may be a familiar place or somewhere totally imaginary. It could be the present day, the past, or even the future. *A Wish after Midnight* by Zetta Elliott sends characters to the 1860s, while *The Hunger Games* by Suzanne Collins takes place in a nightmarish future world. In any story, sensory details help readers see, hear, and feel the setting.

Something has to *happen* in a story—that's what creates the plot. Your characters might solve a mystery, go on a quest, wrestle with an inner conflict, or struggle against other people. Your plot may involve real-life issues such as illness (as with John Green's *The Fault in Our Stars*) or racism (as with *Feathers* by Jacqueline

Woodson). Or your plot may include outrageously silly events such as the factory tour in Roald Dahl's *Charlie and the Chocolate Factory.* Your plot should hook the reader's interest and build suspense about what might happen next.

Works of fiction have a beginning, a middle, and an end. They can be any length, from short stories to novellas and full-length novels. Maybe you're most interested in writing a short story. Or perhaps you'd like to tackle a novel someday. **Fiction spans different genres, or types, including science fiction, fantasy, mystery, romance, and more.** Your story might combine elements of more than one genre. You might set out to entertain readers, make them laugh, or make them think. It's all up to you—you bring your own unique voice, purpose, and experience to the stories you write.

Prepare to take the first steps toward creating fantastic fiction. You'll choose what you want to write about, whether it's a dark fantasy tale, a mind-bending thriller, or a realistic story that borrows from your life. You'll also discover advice on gathering story ideas and developing characters, a setting, and a plot. And you'll move from writing a rough draft to editing, revising, and perfecting your story. You'll even find advice and examples from master writers along the way. Just turn the page to get started!

FINDING STORY IDEAS

Stories rarely pop into a writer's head fully formed. They begin as an idea and grow as an author writes them. Your story might begin with something small. Perhaps a vivid image makes you rush to your keyboard—or maybe you jot down a snappy line of dialogue and start to wonder what sort of character would say it. You might be set on telling a story with a haunting setting. With a little imagination and patience, that fragment can lead to endless possibilities.

LOOK TO YOUR OWN LIFE

When looking for story ideas, do what many writing teachers suggest: write what you know. You may think your life is boring, but dig deep. You'll find you have stories that only you can share. What makes you unique? Can you cook a special dish or play a musical instrument? When have you been embarrassed? Proud? Afraid? Have you ever spilled a secret, told a lie, or broken a bone? Imagine one of your experiences happening to someone else. What details might you change or invent to create a fictional narrative? Don't hesitate to tweak the original idea if you're headed toward an exciting story. Remember, that idea was just a starting point.

Family and friends can also provide good story ideas. Are there any tales your family tells again and again? Maybe your aunt has a hilarious anecdote about something your dad did when he was little. Perhaps you know someone you might describe as "a real character." What are some memorable things this person does or says? You can exaggerate that person's qualities or mix them with others to create a fictional character for your story.

KEEP A WRITER'S NOTEBOOK

Once you start looking for story ideas, you'll find them all around you. Get in the habit of collecting ideas in a writer's notebook. This might be a plain spiral-bound notebook or a hardcover journal. You can also keep a list of ideas on a laptop, a tablet, or a smartphone—anything you can carry with you. When an idea comes to mind, jot it down.

Use your writer's notebook to record what you see and hear. Jot down snippets of conversation overheard on the bus. Sit in

a busy place and note what you see people doing. Someone is carrying a package—what's inside? A couple is holding hands— who are they and where did they meet? Use your imagination to fill in the rest. And keep an eye out for quirky images, such as a lone tennis shoe in the street or an art student toting a papier-mâché moon. These details might make their way into a story.

Don't place limits on what you put in your writer's notebook. You can keep your notebook by your bed so you can record your dreams when you wake up. You can also collect vocabulary words, quotations, news clippings, photos from magazines, or even shopping lists—anything that inspires your writing. Story ideas are everywhere!

READ, READ, READ!

Reading is one of the most important things you can do to become a better writer. When you read, you take in the different rhythms a story can have. You feed your brain with new words or creative uses for terms you already know. Reading can give you new ideas for plot or setting as well. A Sherlock Holmes mystery may inspire you to write your own detective story. A news article about a scientific discovery might lead to a good sci-fi plot.

Reading often—and reading a wide range of books—is also the best way to find the style of writing you like best. When you start writing, you may find yourself imitating your favorite writer's style. Maybe you'll mimic the wit of Dorothy Parker or the stark voice of Ernest Hemingway. It's not wrong to try out another writer's style. Just be careful never to plagiarize, or steal, another writer's words or ideas. Copying and pasting phrases, sentences, or paragraphs from another story is plagiarism, even if you reword or change characters' names or other details.

LEARN FROM THE MASTERS

Story ideas often come while you're busy doing something else. Author J. R. R. Tolkien, a longtime English professor at Oxford University in Oxford, England, came up with the idea for his fantasy novel *The Hobbit* while grading his students' papers. Coming across a blank page, he impulsively scribbled, "In a hole in the ground there lived a hobbit." Tolkien had no idea what a hobbit was, so he had to write a book to find out! The sentence Tolkien wrote became the opening line of his classic book.

Hobbits are small, humanlike creatures in the imaginary world called Middle-Earth. They appear in both *The Hobbit* and *The Lord of the Rings* books and movies.

UNLOCK YOUR CREATIVITY

Gathering ideas for stories is a creative process. It works best when you relax and let your mind roam free. Try brainstorming to unlock the creative side of your mind. Start with a prompt such as "What if . . . ?" or "I remember . . ." Then write down as many responses as you can think of in five minutes. *(I remember . . . my grandmother's hands as she taught me to make dumplings . . . the cold January morning when my little brother was born . . . the sizzling pain of a skinned knee when I fell off my bike at age six.)* Don't reject any ideas. You can also try brainstorming out loud with a writing partner or group. The more ideas, the better!

Clustering works well for visual thinkers. To cluster, write a topic or a theme in the center of a sheet of paper and then circle it. Next, draw a line branching out from the center every time you have an idea related to the topic. A cluster chart about survival might have ideas such as these surrounding the topic: "A kid struggles to survive in a new school"; "Shipwreck survivors search for food"; "Only the children survive a nuclear war."

Freewriting is another technique for generating ideas. Grab your writer's notebook and write down every thought that comes to mind. Don't stop to think; just let your ideas flow freely onto the page. If you get stuck, repeat the same phrase as long as you need to. Here's an example:

OK, I'm writing. What to write about? What to write, what to write. The dog won't stop bugging me. He probably wants to go outside again so he can dig another hole in the yard. What's he digging for? Suppose there's something buried back there.

Continue freewriting for as long as you wish. Keep an open mind during this creative process. As one thought leads to another, you may stumble upon surprising new ideas for your plot, characters, setting, and more.

WRITE IT OUT!

Skim through a copy of your local newspaper (print edition, if possible) with the goal of finding at least ten story ideas. Clip out or take photos of the articles that interest you and place them in your writer's journal. Then choose the best idea and write a short fictional narrative. You can even challenge yourself by writing a story that connects several unrelated items. For example, what might a scientific breakthrough, a basketball player, and a world event have in common?

DEVELOPING CHARACTERS, CONFLICT, AND SETTINGS

Characters are the heart of fiction. Well-written characters become almost like friends to a reader. Think about Bud of *Bud, Not Buddy*, Anne Shirley of *Anne of Green Gables*, or Wilbur the pig of *Charlotte's Web*. Readers may hate to close the book at the end of the story and break contact with these characters. But if a writer fails to develop believable characters, his or her story often falls flat. The plot may have clever twists and turns, but most readers won't care enough about the characters to keep reading.

Characters don't have to be human. Some important characters in fiction take the form of animals. *Charlotte's Web* wouldn't be the same without Wilbur the pig or Charlotte the spider.

Before you jump into writing a story, give yourself time to develop your characters. Start by freewriting about your main character, or protagonist. Get to know this character inside and out. What does he or she look like? How would you describe the character's personality? What are this character's goals, dreams, and secret fears? Invent details about the character's background, including place of birth and past experiences. Even if you don't include this information in your story, you'll have it in the back of your mind as you write.

After developing a protagonist, focus on other characters. Is there an antagonist in your story, someone in conflict with the main character? What does this person want? Then consider other major characters in your protagonist's life, such as a little sister, a best friend, or a wise mentor. Make a list of your characters, jotting down names and descriptions. Writing this list will help you keep track of your characters as you create your story.

WRITE IT OUT!
Are you having trouble fleshing out your protagonist? Write a one-page character sketch. This is a perfect time to get creative. For instance, your character sketch could describe the contents of the character's bedroom. What pictures hang on the walls? What would a reader find in your character's dresser drawer? You could also think about a typical day in the life of your character. Let's say the character writes a to-do list. What items would a reader find on that list?

NAMING YOUR CHARACTERS

Are you looking for ways to make your characters stand out? Choose colorful names that fit their personalities. For inspiration, think of well-known characters from literature. Huckleberry Finn and Oliver Twist have touched many generations of readers. Their distinctive names help make them memorable. The same is true of a more recent character such as Pi Patel.

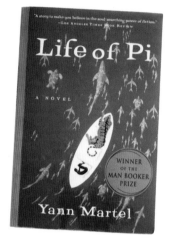

Consider using a name with a particular meaning. Sandra Cisneros, author of *The House on Mango Street*, named her main character Esperanza. This word means "hope" in Spanish. The name also fits the character, a girl with hopes and dreams.

If your story is set in the past or in a different part of the world, you might need to do some research before naming your characters. Go online or head to a library to find names that suit the time and the location of your story. Ancient cultures might even inspire the names used in a science fiction or fantasy story. J. R. R. Tolkien used names from Norse mythology in *The Lord of the Rings*. Suzanne Collins used the names of ancient Romans for characters in *The Hunger Games*.

SHOW AND TELL

Characterization is the act of creating or describing your character. Writers do this by describing a character's appearance, inner thoughts, actions, and words. They may also reveal what others say or think about the character. Good writers don't only *tell* what a character is like; they *show* it. Consider the difference between these two paragraphs:

1. *Payton McKinley was tall and skinny. He was insecure and bullied other kids. Nobody liked him.*
2. *Payton McKinley was a beanpole of a boy. He had grown so fast that his sleeves were too short and he got dizzy whenever he looked down. When other kids gaped at his size, Payton dribbled their heads and dunked them into their lockers. Everyone rolled their eyes and turned their backs when he swaggered down the hall.*

In the second paragraph, the writer never tells the reader that Payton is tall and skinny. Instead, the writer uses the term *beanpole* to help readers create a mental picture. The details about Payton's sleeves and his dizziness enhance the idea. Instead of telling the reader that Payton is an insecure bully, the writer shows Payton in action, leaving the reader to reach his or her own conclusions. The image of people rolling their eyes and turning their backs shows, rather than tells, what others think about Payton.

Since showing often requires longer, more descriptive passages, you won't want to "show" all the time. There will be times when it's better to just quickly tell the reader certain information. Use your judgment to create a mixture of showing and telling about your character.

WRITING DIALOGUE

Dialogue is another good way to show what characters feel or think. For example, rather than telling readers that other students are sick of Payton, you could show it in dialogue:

"Look out—here comes the next LeBron James!"
Payton hollered, shoving his way down the hall. A fifth
grader bounced into a wastebasket.
"You're a jerk," someone behind him muttered. It
was Malik, from homeroom.
Payton froze. "What did you call me?"

To write dialogue, start a new paragraph for each speaker. Enclose the speaker's words in quotation marks, followed by a tagline such as "she said" or "he asked" when needed, to indicate who is speaking. You can use more specific verbs such as *whispered* or *snapped* to indicate the way someone speaks, but most of the time, stick with simple verbs such as *said, asked,* or *shouted.* The focus should be on what the character says.

Dialogue should sound natural, but it doesn't need to imitate speech exactly. Don't include *ums* and *uhs* or ellipses points (. . .) every time a character pauses. Even though that's the way people actually speak, dialogue written that way can be difficult to read. And be consistent. If a character uses phrases such as "I ain't," or "y'all," avoid having the same character say "I am not" or "all of you" a few lines later. Readers can't grasp a character's personality through dialogue if the character's way of speaking keeps changing.

CREATING THREE-DIMENSIONAL CHARACTERS

One-dimensional characters can drag down a work of fiction. Think of the snobby cheerleader, the fearless hero, the dumb jock, the crabby librarian, or the absentminded professor. These characters are familiar, but they aren't very interesting. They have a single dominant characteristic. That's not realistic. Believable characters are multidimensional—that is, they have many qualities. They should also change over the course of the story.

If you recognize one-dimensional characters in your story, make them come to life by hinting at what they think and feel. Reveal their motivation for acting as they do. For instance, does the snobby cheerleader have her own fears and insecurities? Does the fearless hero have any selfish habits? You might also give characters unexpected qualities that don't fit the cliché. **Maybe the jock loves botany, or the librarian is crabby because you interrupted her game of** *Minecraft.* Even a wicked villain should have more than one dimension. It makes for a better story if we know his or her background—what made the villain so twisted? Does the villain have a weakness or a secret love?

Not all of your characters need to show numerous dimensions. After all, J. K. Rowling does not give readers the name or the motivation of every character at Hogwarts. The purpose of some characters is to flesh out the setting, further the action, or show the main character's personality. But make sure your main character and other major characters have depth.

IDENTIFYING CONFLICT

A compelling story must involve some kind of conflict. Conflict is what drives a plot. Most stories introduce a conflict at the beginning, build up to a climax (high point) near the end of the story, and show that the conflict has been resolved at the end. The main character will have achieved a goal, won or lost a battle, solved a mystery, or learned to accept a painful truth. This change, whether epic or subtle, completes the story. If there is no conflict, there is no change. And without change, there is no plot.

Conflict may be internal or external. An internal conflict takes place inside a character's mind. A character's struggle to choose between right and wrong is an example of an internal conflict. An external conflict positions the character against a force in the outside world, such as a friend, a school, or a harsh environment. A character may struggle to stand out, search for acceptance, or rebel against injustice. In an adventure story such as *The Call of the Wild* by Jack London, characters battle the forces of nature. In fantasy stories, they may battle monsters, sorcerers, or other evil creatures.

Stories often include several conflicts. Identify possible conflicts in your story. Are they internal or external? What is the central conflict, and how will you introduce it? Once you've made your decision, think about possible events in your story. How will these events bring the conflict to a climax? Freewrite or brainstorm to find possible answers to these questions.

THINK ABOUT THEME

Outlining a conflict may also help you discover your story's theme. A theme is a central idea in a literary work. For instance, Veronica Roth's futuristic novel *Divergent* and Walter Mosely's *47* share a common theme: the search for identity. Common themes of fiction include the importance of friendship, the difficulties of growing up, the destructiveness of hate, or the power of love.

Your story may not have any one obvious theme. Don't struggle to come up with one. Just keep the idea of theme in the back of your mind. If there is a theme in your tale, it will emerge as you write.

DESCRIBING THE SETTING

The setting of your story includes the time and the place in which it happens. It's your job to describe the setting for the reader. If your setting is a place you know well, your job is easier. However, what if you've never been there? Then do some research. Paris, France, may be a perfect setting for a romantic story, but you can't transport readers there with one mention of the Eiffel Tower.

If you've picked out a real but unfamiliar place, check out a travel guide that describes the location in detail. Let's say you're set on that story about Paris. Read a map so you can trace your character's path through the city. Learn the names of streets, parks, cafés, and *Métro* (subway) stops. Look at photos so you can describe the cars people drive or what businesses you might see on a typical street.

If your story is set in the past, consult books about what life was like during the time period you've chosen. Read up on the fashions of that era so you can accurately depict period clothing—doublet

Readers will need more than a mention of the Eiffel Tower to understand the setting of your Paris-based story.

In her short story "Rules of the Game," author Amy Tan (below) describes the sights, sounds, smells, and textures of her setting: "We lived in San Francisco's Chinatown . . . in a warm, clean, two-bedroom flat that sat above a small Chinese bakery specializing in steamed

pastries and dim sum. In the early morning, when the alley was still quiet, I could smell fragrant red beans as they were cooked down to a pasty sweetness. By daybreak, our flat was heavy with the odor of fried sesame balls and sweet curried chicken crescents. From my bed, I would listen as my father got ready for work, then locked the door behind him, one-two-three clicks."

and codpiece or waistcoat and breeches? A detail that doesn't fit the time period might take your readers out of the story. For instance, a medieval knight can't use current slang or heat up a taco in the microwave—unless you're going for comedy!

Science fiction and fantasy settings require imagination and planning. Although sci-fi worlds are imaginary, they need to seem real. Create a list of rules about what is and isn't possible in your world. For instance, does your planet have gravity? If a character has magical powers, what are the limits to these powers? You may need to invent new words for concepts that don't exist in our world. To help the reader picture these unfamiliar things, compare them with something familiar: *The captain navigated through a grove of* arboliads, *treelike creatures whose arms twisted around the ship.*

Whatever your setting, make it real to readers by using sensory details. These details appeal to the senses of sight, sound, smell, taste, and touch. With the right words, you can create a particular mood, or atmosphere, within your setting. For instance, the description of a house in a romance would be very different from that in a horror story:

1. *The mansion sat like a wedding cake atop a green hill.*
2. *The mansion loomed on the moor, emerging from the mist like a ghostly ship.*

Vivid word choices can transport readers wherever you want to take them and make them see, hear, and feel the world of your characters.

WRITE IT OUT!
To practice creating a sense of place, pick a location and describe it using a series of sensory details. What mood do you want to create? Next, write a second description of the same place. This time, use details that create a completely different mood. For instance, you might describe a path through the woods, first to create a peaceful mood and then a mood of fear.

CHAPTER 3

MAKING A WRITING MAP

Until now, you've been freewriting: letting your thoughts wander down different avenues, meeting a dead end or two, and circling back. This process is an essential part of creating a story. Once you've sketched out your story's characters, conflict, and setting, you're ready to make a map. Your writing map might be a simple outline of the story's beginning, middle, and end. Or the map might take the form of a plot diagram, a timeline, or a storyboard—anything that helps you visualize the events of your narrative.

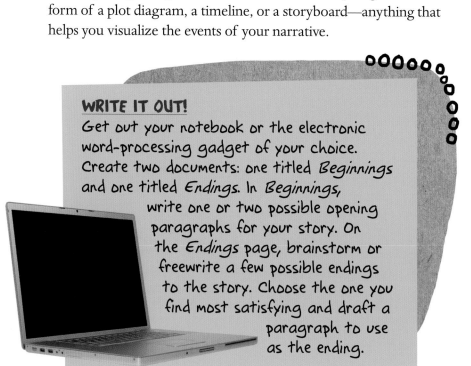

WRITE IT OUT!
Get out your notebook or the electronic word-processing gadget of your choice. Create two documents: one titled *Beginnings* and one titled *Endings*. In *Beginnings*, write one or two possible opening paragraphs for your story. On the *Endings* page, brainstorm or freewrite a few possible endings to the story. Choose the one you find most satisfying and draft a paragraph to use as the ending.

MAPPING A BEGINNING, A MIDDLE, AND AN END

To visualize your plot in a simple way, create a map of the story's beginning, middle, and end. You might not know all the details yet, but outline what you can. First, jot down a possible title for your story. Note the main character, setting, and conflict. Then jot down your idea for the first lines or the first scene of the story. Consider a "hook" that grabs readers, such as a startling image or a sweeping description of a scene. Another trick is to start in the middle of the action—*in medias res*, to use the fancy Latin term—and then flash back to explain what led to that moment. Here's an example of an *in medias res* opening:

> *The cyborgs circled, their metallic minds buzzing, their electric eyes searching. I couldn't believe I had let myself get into this situation. In a rush, my mind flashed back to what I had done wrong.*

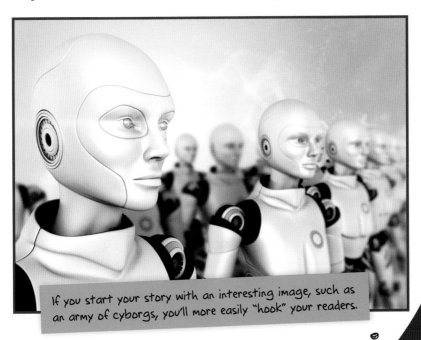

If you start your story with an interesting image, such as an army of cyborgs, you'll more easily "hook" your readers.

Next, list events that will happen in the middle of the story, as the action heats up. Finally, write down a possible ending for the story. You can base your map on this example:

Possible Title: Right on Time
Main Character: Rafael, a 16-year-old boy
Setting: Minneapolis in the present day and in the year 3050
Conflict: Rafael must avoid danger and search for a way back from a time warp.
Beginning Hook: Open with Rafael being surrounded by cyborgs as he attempts to return to his era.
Middle (action heating up): Describe how Rafael slipped into the time warp and landed in the future. He meets characters who help him and some who threaten him.
End: Rafael is surrounded but he manages to escape.

LEARN FROM THE MASTERS

The first few lines of Toni Cade Bambara's short story "The War of the Wall" introduce the story's main characters and the central conflict. Can you identify those parts from the lines below?

"Me and Lou had no time for courtesies. We were late for school. So we just flat out told the painter lady to quit messing with the wall. It was our wall, and she had no right coming into our neighborhood painting on it."

CREATE A PLOT DIAGRAM

A plot diagram is another way to map your story. This tool helps you divide your story into five parts: exposition, rising action, climax, falling action, and resolution. These parts of the story create an arc or pyramid shape. Looking back to this diagram as you write might help you pace your story or decide how much space you devote to each section.

Make exposition the first point on your plot diagram. Exposition includes a description or an explanation of the characters, the setting, and the plot. In a short story, the exposition might fill the first paragraph or two. In a novel, it could take up the first chapter or more. A story's exposition often introduces the main conflict or the goal of the piece. A specific event, called the inciting incident, might make this conflict obvious. If you like, summarize the exposition of your story on your diagram, noting the central conflict and how you will introduce it.

The next section of your plot diagram covers the story's rising action. This is where the plot thickens, or becomes more complicated. In a mystery, your character might be finding clues. In a romance, the characters might have a series of misunderstandings. A problem worsens, new information comes to light, or unexpected obstacles get in the way of a character's goal. These complications should lead readers to wonder what will happen next. If you've thought of the complications that will happen in your story, note them in this area of your plot diagram.

A pyramid-style writing map is especially useful for visualizing the next part of your story: the moment when rising action gives way to the climax. Mark the climax at the high point of your plot

WRITERS ON WRITING

Plot pyramids, storyboards, and timelines work well for many writers. But don't feel bad if you prefer not to use these tools. Lois Lowry (below), author of *The Giver* and *Number the Stars*, writes without a map. "Careful planning doesn't work for me as a writer," she says. "If I try to make an outline (and I have)—I usually lose interest in the book. . . . A lot of the fun and excitement of writing, for me, is because of the surprise of it: each day in the creation of a book is a new adventure for me, and that wouldn't be true if I had a set of index cards telling me what was supposed to happen next."

pyramid. It is the moment everything has been building toward. By charting the events of your story along a plot pyramid, you can make sure the climax doesn't happen too early. What is the "big moment" of the story? Label it on your diagram.

Your plot diagram should include a downward slope following the climax. Label this part of the story the falling action. In many stories, things begin falling into place for the main character during this section. Falling action ends with the story's resolution, or the point where the main conflict has ceased.

Falling action and a resolution are often satisfying parts of a story, but they are rarely as gripping as the rising action. So use your plot diagram to see that these sections don't take up too much space in your story. To identify the falling action, ask yourself: What will have changed in your story after the climax? Note some of this info on your diagram too. Before you begin, check out this model plot diagram:

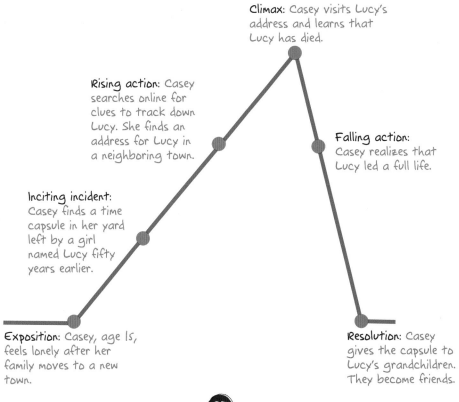

Climax: Casey visits Lucy's address and learns that Lucy has died.

Rising action: Casey searches online for clues to track down Lucy. She finds an address for Lucy in a neighboring town.

Falling action: Casey realizes that Lucy led a full life.

Inciting incident: Casey finds a time capsule in her yard left by a girl named Lucy fifty years earlier.

Exposition: Casey, age 15, feels lonely after her family moves to a new town.

Resolution: Casey gives the capsule to Lucy's grandchildren. They become friends.

CREATING A TIMELINE OR A STORYBOARD

Timelines and storyboards are two other tools for mapping the events in a story. A timeline can help you keep track of the chronology, or the order of events, in your story. This type of map is especially useful if your story takes place over a long period of time or if you plan to use flashbacks that tell about earlier events. Here's an example:

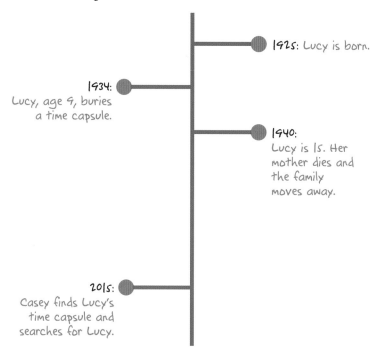

1925: Lucy is born.

1934: Lucy, age 9, buries a time capsule.

1940: Lucy is 15. Her mother dies and the family moves away.

2015: Casey finds Lucy's time capsule and searches for Lucy.

A storyboard breaks a story down into distinct scenes or events. Draw a series of boxes. In each box, draw a picture or write a few sentences to describe an event. You can also create a movable storyboard using index cards. Create one card for each story event, and then spread the cards on a table. You can move them around to change the order of events. You can also refer to your storyboard when you write your first draft, writing a paragraph or so based on each box.

Casey has been depressed since moving to a new house. She stares out the window at her dog digging in the yard.

Something is buried—a suitcase. Casey digs it out and opens it. The suitcase contains a sketchbook, crocheted lace, a photograph, etc.

Casey pores over the contents and finds clues about a girl named Lucy. She wonders if Lucy is still alive.

Look over your storyboard. Do you need to change direction to avoid a roadblock? Pull over to check out the scenery? Make a detour for character development? For instance, the example above needs a description of Casey's house, a backstory about why her family moved there, and scenes depicting her family. You can easily create new boards for new scenes. Your map is just a guide. Feel free to change it as you go.

WRITING A *REALLY* ROUGH DRAFT

As you sit down to write your rough draft, the blank white page in front of you can be daunting. Relax. Remember that this is a *really* rough draft. You could even call it a "discovery draft." This is your opportunity to experiment with point of view and voice. Discover what works and what doesn't. Don't worry about grammar, spelling, and punctuation. Also, try not to revise your writing as you go. Sometimes your first impulse is the correct one, and the more you stop to edit, the more uncertain you will feel. Just get it all out on paper!

POINT OF VIEW

Now that you've mapped out the events of your story, you should have a good idea of the story's shape and direction. But before you write your first draft, you must decide exactly how you'll tell it. First, consider point of view. Is one of your characters telling the story, using the pronoun *I*? If so, your story uses the first-person point of view. If the narrator is not one of the characters in the story and uses *he, she,* and *they*—but not *I*—to describe the action, the story is in the third-person point of view.

Next, consider how close your narrator is to the story. An omniscient, or all-knowing, narrator tells the story as if looking

down from above. A completely omniscient narrator can see any event and know what all characters are thinking. This type of narrator is able to say things such as, "Meanwhile, on the other side of town. . . ." A limited narrator follows one character's point of view. The narrator reveals the inner thoughts and feelings of that character but doesn't share what other characters are thinking or feeling. (Some writers put the focus on different characters from chapter to chapter. Popular authors such as Jonathan Franzen and Zadie Smith have featured this approach in their novels.)

Most stories are told from the first-person or third-person limited point of view. These points of view both allow readers to focus on just one character, digging deep into that character's mind and motivations. Each approach has different advantages. The first-person point of view is a good choice if your character has a distinct personality or a unique way of speaking that you want to convey. Here's an example:

So Ike and me see all this cash piled on Jimmy's desk. I'm like, whoa. Ike gives me this look, like "Don't you dare take anything."

The first-person narrative can be difficult to maintain because a writer must stay "in character" for the entire story. The third-person limited can be an easier choice because it tells the story as seen from one person's point of view but not in that person's own words. Check out this version of the cash-on-desk scene from earlier, retold in the third-person limited:

Carla sucked in her breath. They could take a few bills and he would never know. Then she felt Ike's eyes on her. "Don't you dare take anything," he said.

The omniscient narrator is a good choice for large, sweeping stories that feature multiple characters, settings, and conflicts. It is the point of view used in works such as *War and Peace* by Leo Tolstoy and *One Hundred Years of Solitude* by Gabriel García Márquez. This point of view can also allow for feelings of irony or anticipation, because the narrator can let a reader know things that the characters don't know. Here's another version of the cash-on-desk scene as told by an omniscient narrator:

Ike and Carla eyed the cash, both tempted to take the bait. Neither of them guessed that someone was watching their every move.

Write your draft using whichever point of view feels most natural, but keep the narrator's voice consistent—don't "head-hop" from one point of view to another. Remember to consider point of view as you visualize the action or the setting of the story. Describe what your point-of-view character can see, hear, feel, and think. This will help the story come alive for the reader.

LEARN FROM THE MASTERS

In the first-person limited point of view, a character tells a story in his or her own words. Sometimes that narrator is someone readers shouldn't trust. The narrator of Edgar Allan Poe's horror classic short story "The Tell-Tale Heart" claims he is perfectly sane—but read this passage and see if you agree:

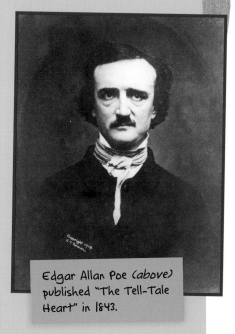

Edgar Allan Poe (above) published "The Tell-Tale Heart" in 1843.

> True!—nervous—very, very dreadfully nervous I had been and am; but why will you say that I am mad? . . . I heard all things in the heaven and in the earth. I heard many things in hell. How, then, am I mad? Hearken! and observe how healthily—how calmly I can tell you the whole story. . . . I loved the old man. He had never wronged me. He had never given me insult. For his gold I had no desire. I think it was his eye! Yes, it was this! He had the eye of a vulture—a pale blue eye, with a film over it. Whenever it fell upon me, my blood ran cold; and so by degrees—very gradually—I made up my mind to take the life of the old man, and thus rid myself of the eye forever.

FINDING THE RIGHT VOICE

A writer brings personality to the voice of a narrator through word choice and sentence structure. Your story's narrative voice could be funny, chatty, ironic, sincere, serious, or playful, and so on. The voice of a narrator is often more obvious in stories told in the first-person point of view, because a character is sharing the story in his or her own words. That character's attitude colors the entire story. But an omniscient narrator can have a distinctive voice too.

Different genres of fiction tend to feature different voices. The voice you use to tell the story of a romance might be lighter than the voice you use for a horror story. If you're tackling a serious subject, you can lighten your story through voice. In his novel *The Absolutely True Diary of a Part-Time Indian*, author Sherman Alexie

WRITERS ON WRITING

Even successful authors sometimes struggle to get their first draft on the page. Lisa Yee, author of *Millicent Min, Girl Genius*, once needed a special object to cure her writer's block. "One time I couldn't write until I had a sock monkey," she commented on a friend's blog. "I know it sounds weird now, but I swear the lack of a sock monkey shut me down." Follow Yee's example and find a special object to inspire your writing. Place it on your desk so you can look at it whenever you feel blocked.

Hazel Grace Lancaster of *The Fault in Our Stars,* played by Shailene Woodley in the film adaptation (above), is a narrator with a strong personality and a striking sense of humor.

depicts characters struggling with poverty, alcoholism, bullying, and discrimination. But the voice of his hilarious narrator, Arnold Spirit Jr., keeps the weight of these serious issues from becoming overwhelming. Hazel, the narrator of *The Fault in Our Stars*, uses a darkly humorous tone when discussing her experiences as a teen with cancer. In the novel *Frankenstein*, author Mary Shelley uses the regretful voice of scientist Victor Frankenstein to ground her outlandish story in human emotions.

If you're having trouble settling on voice and tone at the start of your story, stick with the third-person limited point of view. This point of view can feature a fairly neutral voice. The story's characters will express themselves through their dialogue and their actions. You could also pick the first-person point of view and write the story as if you were telling it to a friend. The story might come out more naturally if you don't force yourself into a particular voice or style.

SETTING THE SCENE AND KEEPING THE STORY MOVING

Even if you don't have an idea for an exciting opening to your story, try to dive in and start writing. You can go back and add something better later on. Your story's opening should set the scene, introducing readers to the setting and main characters. Refer to your story map. What is your main conflict? Be sure you introduce that early in the story as well.

As you move onto the middle part of the story, continue to use your story map as a guide to scenes you want to include. Identify the purpose of each scene you outlined. Focus on scenes that add obstacles or build suspense. Use transitional phrases such as *an hour later* or *the next Saturday* to shift from scene to scene. And avoid unnecessary details that might drag out a story. You wouldn't want to write a scene about your main character brushing his or her teeth—unless it helps the plot move forward.

ENDING STRONG

While putting together your story map, you identified a possible ending for your story. But during the drafting process, your story may have changed direction. Does the ending you envisioned still work? If not, don't feel bound to it. Draft one or two endings if you like. And remember, endings can be tricky. Sometimes they're the hardest section to write. So if you're creating a story on a deadline—or just a timetable you've set for yourself—leave plenty of time for this part.

Many strong endings give readers the feeling that all the story's elements have fallen into place. Even if you want to surprise readers, don't introduce a new detail from out of nowhere. Think back to an example on page 24: the map about "Right on Time," a story in which a boy faces off against cyborgs. Let's say the boy, Rafael, learns that his antique pocket watch is actually a time machine, and he uses the time machine to escape. Readers should not learn about the watch for the first time as the story reaches its climax. A really satisfying version of "Right on Time" might mention the pocket watch once or twice early on—while saving the watch's secret for the end.

CHAPTER 5

REVISING YOUR STORY

Revision is the process of making changes to improve a writing piece. When you revise, you give your story a second (or third or fourth) look. You can add, delete, move, or replace words, lines, and passages. The revision stage is an opportunity to strengthen characterization, build suspense in the plot, and adjust the flow of your narrative. Before you revise your rough draft, set it aside for a few days. When you return, you will see it from a fresh perspective.

ANOTHER PAIR OF EYES (OR TWO)

Getting feedback from others can help you evaluate your story. Find two people to read your story and offer a critique. Since you'll want different perspectives, consider asking one person your age and one adult. Next, skim through the story and run a spell-check to catch any typos. Print out several copies and make sure the font and the spacing allow for an easy read. Give your readers a list of questions you would like to have answered, such as the following:

1. *Characters: Are the characters well rounded? Are their actions and dialogue believable?*

Ask a friend or a classmate to read your rough draft. You can use his or her notes to improve the final version of your story.

2. Setting: Is the setting vivid? Does the story include too much description of the setting or not enough?

3. Sequence of events: Are the story's events easy to follow? Is the pace too slow or too fast in certain areas?

4. Plot: Does the beginning hook the reader? Is the ending satisfying?

5. Voice, tone, and point of view: Do the voice and tone suit the story? Is the point of view consistent?

6. Theme: What do you think is the overall theme of the story?

Invite readers to put a star next to passages they think are strong, squiggly lines under passages that don't work well, or a question mark next to passages they find confusing. Try not to take any criticism personally. If you don't agree with the reviewer's suggestions, feel free to ignore them or ask someone else! After all, it's your story.

After receiving feedback, pinpoint areas for improvement based on your reviewers' suggestions. Then take another look at your story to evaluate it for yourself. Print out a clean copy and read it aloud. Does the story flow well? Which parts of the story do you like best? Circle or underline words, sentences, or paragraphs you would like to improve.

REVIEW CHARACTERIZATION AND DESCRIPTION

When you revise your story, find ways to strengthen characterization. If a character strikes you as flat, add or rewrite dialogue to reveal his or her motivation—or just to give more glimpses into the character's personality. The revision stage is your time to check that your creations have strong, distinct identities. Read your dialogue aloud with a partner. Does it sound natural? Does it fit the personality of the character who is speaking? If not, make some revisions.

The revision stage also gives you a chance to look closely at your descriptive language. Have you used certain words and phrases too often? Are you telling instead of showing? Replace bland words such as *beautiful* and *exciting* with more vivid adjectives such as *radiant* or *electrifying*. **Look for clichés such as "It was pitch-black outside" or "He was mad as a hornet."** Unless these clichés are part of the way your narrator speaks, use fresher imagery.

When possible, use precise nouns and verbs—instead of *tree*, write *elm*. Instead of *walked*, write *crept*, *sauntered*, or *shuffled*. Get rid of *very* and *really*. If someone is *really angry*, why not say she is *irate*? Better yet, show the reader what irate looks like: "Her lips narrowed, and she clenched her fists."

LEARN FROM THE MASTERS

In Langston Hughes's short story "Thank You, M'am," a woman catches hold of a boy who has just tried to steal her purse. Note the way in which Hughes mixes the characters' dialogue with their actions in the text below. Can you "see" the action? Can you "hear" the characters' voices?

Langston Hughes (above) published the short story "Thank You, M'am" in 1958.

"Lady, I'm sorry," whispered the boy.

"Um-hum! Your face is dirty. I got a great mind to wash your face for you. Ain't you got nobody home to tell you to wash your face?"

"No'm," said the boy.

"Then it will get washed this evening," said the large woman, starting up the street, dragging the frightened boy behind her.

He looked as if he were fourteen or fifteen, frail and willow-wild, in tennis shoes and blue jeans.

The woman said, "You ought to be my son. I would teach you right from wrong. Least I can do right now is to wash your face. Are you hungry?"

"No'm," said the being-dragged boy. "I just want you to turn me loose."

IMPROVE FLOW, PACE, AND POINT OF VIEW

When revising your story, read through it once with a focus on how it flows. If your story has too much action, it might feel rushed. If it has too much description, it might feel too slow. A story with too much of either could also seem cramped. Find the right balance among the story's action scenes, descriptive passages, and dialogue. If the story's pace drags in certain places, making cuts can help speed it up. For instance, you could get rid of repetitive words or phrases. If your original lines read, *The woods were dark. It was so dark the boys couldn't see their own feet,* you could shorten it to, *The woods were so dark, the boys couldn't see their own feet.*

If you don't think a scene is moving at the right speed, try to vary the length and structure of your sentences. Use short sentences and phrases to speed up the pace in suspenseful scenes. Use long, complex sentences when you want to slow the pace and create a more thoughtful mood.

Also take the opportunity to scan your story for mistakes in point of view. Sometimes writers using the first-person or third-person limited point of view describe something that the point-of-view character cannot know or see. For instance, *I stomped up to my room and slammed the door. My parents didn't move to follow me. They stayed put and rolled their eyes.* What's wrong with this passage? The character can't see her parents rolling their eyes after she slams the door!

EDITING YOUR STORY

After making revisions to your story, print out a clean copy. Proofread it, checking for errors in spelling, word usage, grammar, and mechanics. Reading the story aloud might help the process.

LEARN FROM THE MASTERS

The legendary British author Charles Dickens starts off his coming-of-age novel *Great Expectations* with a suspenseful scene. An escaped convict seizes Pip, a young orphan. Dickens uses sentence fragments, punctuated by commas, to create a rapid pace that mimics Pip's terrified thoughts:

Charles Dickens *(above)* published *Great Expectations* in 1861.

"Keep still, you little devil, or I'll cut your throat!"

A fearful man, all in coarse gray, with a great iron on his leg. A man with no hat, and with broken shoes, and with an old rag tied round his head. A man who had been soaked in water, and smothered in mud, and lamed by stones, and cut by flints, and stung by nettles, and torn by briars; who limped, and shivered, and glared, and growled; and whose teeth chattered in his head as he seized me by the chin.

"Oh! Don't cut my throat, sir," I pleaded in terror. "Pray don't do it, sir."

Most word-processing programs have a spelling and grammar checker. Such a tool can help you catch most spelling errors, but it won't necessarily catch all of them. For instance, it may miss mistakes in word usage such as using *you're* in place of *your*. Pay attention to words you frequently misspell. Make an effort to memorize the spelling so you don't have to rely on a spelling and grammar checker too often.

While proofreading your story, stay on the lookout for mistakes in verb tense or subject-and-verb agreement. Can you spot what's wrong with the following line? *I stomp up to my room and slammed the door.* What about this one? *My parents always says I'm too dramatic.* These kinds of missteps can take readers out of your story.

WRITERS ON WRITING

Veronica Roth (below), author of the *Divergent* series, shares advice she once received from a writing teacher:

Imagine that you are about to embark upon a twenty mile hike through the wilderness, and you have to fit everything you need into one backpack. Do you want to bring your hair dryer? Uh, no. . . . [O]nly take what you absolutely need to make it to the end of the hike. And it's the same in writing. Do we need to know what your character eats at a given meal? Not unless someone chokes on a cherry pit or has an allergic reaction to the shellfish.

In fiction, rules about mechanics are not as strict as they might be for a school report. Writers sometimes use incomplete sentences to create a mood or set a pace. But if you give this a try, make sure the result does not confuse the reader. Note the difference between these two examples:

1. *I watched. Waited. Nothing.*
2. *She ran smack into. A lady waiting for the bus.*

The first example features incomplete sentences, but it isn't hard for the reader to follow. In the second example, the reader might wonder whether "she" ran into the lady or whether the story has left out some information.

PRESENTING YOUR WORK

When your story is complete, find a way to share it! Many national publications, online and in print, accept work by young writers. If you're thirteen or younger, check out *Stone Soup* magazine at www.stonesoup.com to submit your story. Visit *Teen Ink* magazine at www.teenink.com if you are older than thirteen. You and your friends could also start your own literary magazine. You can read your story aloud with friends at an open mic night or even adapt it into reader's theater. Once you've shared your work, keep writing! Many more fantastic fiction stories are just waiting to be told.

WRITING FOR A LIVING

When you think of a fiction writer, what do you picture? Is it a novelist typing away in a rustic cabin, hair disheveled, glasses on crooked? Maybe he or she is going a little nuts from all the solitude and rejection letters. There is some truth to this image. Novels take a long time to write. In fact, fiction writing of any sort requires discipline, passion, and a thick skin. However, this image of the struggling novelist does not represent the vast majority of professional writers.

First of all, few writers are full-time novelists. Many writers share their work with readers through publishing houses but also work in the academic world as teachers of writing, literature, world languages, communications, or other subjects. Teachers may take advantage of long summer holidays to devote themselves to writing. The combination of writing and teaching may be ideal for you if you love working with people and are enthusiastic about sharing your knowledge of the writing craft.

Fiction writers also work in the news media and the book publishing world. Some fiction writers have jobs as journalists. Some work as book editors. If you enjoy critiquing, revising, and editing, you could be a natural for the job of editor. Editors do much more than correct typos and bad grammar—they develop, revise, rewrite, and polish fiction manuscripts selected for publication.

Some creative writers find spots in the world of advertising and marketing. Advertisements rely on vivid images and believable narratives. If you're an avid gamer, you know that a good story is key for many video games. Could a job writing video-game scripts be in your future?

If you do decide to write novels, self-publishing options—both print and electronic—make it easier than ever to share your novel with others. However, what if you're not sure you want to write a full-length novel? Then you might try short stories. A wide variety of print and online magazines accept short fiction. Either way, read as widely as you can and write as often as you can. Take literature and creative writing classes to learn about the craft. Even if you don't aspire to become a professional writer, your writing skills will help you succeed in any career you choose.

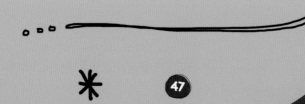

SOURCE NOTES

7 Stephen King, quoted in Zachary Petit, "13 Stephen King Quotes on Writing: Your Moment of Friday Zen," *Writer's Digest*, March 9, 2012, http://www.writersdigest.com/editor-blogs/there-are-no-rules/13-stephen-king-quotes-on-writing-your-moment-of-friday-zen.

8 "Madeleine L'Engle Interview Transcript," *Scholastic,* accessed January 12, 2015, http://www.scholastic.com/teachers/article/madeleine-l39engle-interview-transcript.

9 J. R. R. Tolkien, *The Hobbit* (Boston: Houghton Mifflin, 2012), 5.

20 Amy Tan, "Waverly Jong: Rules of the Game," chap. 5 in *The Joy Luck Club (*New York: Penguin, 2006), 89–90.

24 Toni Cade Bambara, "The War of the Wall," in *Deep Sightings and Rescue Missions: Fiction, Essays and Conversations* (New York: Pantheon, 1996), 57.

26 "Lois Lowry on Her Writing Process—and the One Change She Would Make to *The Giver*," *Write for Kids,* accessed January 12, 2015, http://writeforkids.org/2014/08/lois-lowry-on-her-writing-process-and-the-one-change-she-would-make-to-the-giver/.

31 Ray Bradbury, quoted in Zachary Petit, "21 Ray Bradbury Quotes: Your Moment of Friday Writing Zen," *Writer's Digest,* February 17, 2012, http://www.writersdigest.com/editor-blogs/there-are-no-rules/21-ray-bradbury-quotes-your-moment-of-friday-writing-zen.

33 Edgar Allan Poe, "The Tell-Tale Heart," *The Collected Tales and Poems of Edgar Allan Poe* (New York: Modern Library, 1992), 303.

34 Lisa Yee, comment on "Found it!—Robin," *The Disco Mermaids* (blog), August 19, 2007, http://discomermaids.blogspot.com /2007/08/found-it-robin.html.

41 Langston Hughes, "Thank You, M'am," *The Short Stories of Langston Hughes* (New York: Hill and Wang, 1996), 224.

43 Charles Dickens, *Great Expectations* (New York: Hurd and Houghton, 1867), also available at Project Gutenberg, accessed January 12, 2015, http://www.gutenberg.org /files/1400/1400-h/1400-h.htm.

44 Veronica Roth, "Things I've Learned: The Backpack," *Veronica Roth* (blog), January 14, 2010, http://veronicarothbooks .blogspot.com/2010/01/things-ive-learned-backpack.html.

GLOSSARY

anecdote: a short narrative, often of an informal or biographical nature or both

character: a person or sometimes an animal or another being that is part of the action of a story

cliché: an overused situation or expression

conflict: a problem or a struggle that a character faces throughout a story

dialogue: the words spoken by characters in a story

fiction: writing about imaginary people and events. Forms of fiction include short stories, novels, and novellas.

irony: the opposite of what's expected, or the use of language to express a thought or a feeling by stating the opposite

narrative: a piece of writing that tells a story. Narratives typically have a beginning, a middle, and an end.

plot: the series of events in a story

point of view: the perspective from which a story is told. The first-person point of view and the third-person point of view are both common in fiction.

setting: the time and place of a story

voice: the personality of the narrator, which includes tone and attitude

SELECTED BIBLIOGRAPHY

Bell, James Scott. *Revision & Self-Editing*. Cincinnati: Writer's Digest, 2008.

Cane, William. *Write Like the Masters: Emulating the Best of Hemingway, Faulkner, Salinger, and Others*. Cincinnati: Writer's Digest, 2009.

Cuddon, J. A., and M. A. R. Habib. *The Penguin Dictionary of Literary Terms and Literary Theory*. New York: Penguin, 2014.

Gardner, John. *The Art of Fiction: Notes on Craft for Young Writers*. New York: Vintage, 1991.

King, Stephen. *On Writing: A Memoir of the Craft*. New York: Scribner, 2000.

Kress, Nancy. *Beginnings, Middles, & Ends*. Rev. ed. Cincinnati: Writer's Digest, 2011.

Lamott, Anne. *Bird by Bird: Some Instructions on Writing and Life*. New York: Anchor, 1995.

Lyon, Elizabeth. *A Writer's Guide to Fiction*. New York: Penguin, 2004.

FURTHER INFORMATION

Baby Names
> http://ssa.gov/OACT/babynames
> The Social Security Administration keeps records of the names that were most popular in the United States for each year, beginning in 1880. Check their database to find names for characters of many different eras.

Braun, Eric. *John Green: Star Author, Vlogbrother, and Nerdfighter.* Minneapolis: Lerner Publications, 2015. John Green thought being a writer was an impossible dream. Then he realized writers are just ordinary people. Learn how the best-selling author of *The Fault in Our Stars* made his dreams a reality.

Kellner, Hank. *Write What You See: 99 Photos to Inspire Writing.* Fort Collins, CO: Cottonwood, 2009. Every picture tells a story. When you're struggling to come up with a story idea, find inspiration in one of the ninety-nine photos collected in this book.

National Novel Writing Month
> http://nanowrimo.org
> November is National Novel Writing Month. Think you can write a fifty-thousand-word novel in thirty days? Visit this website to take the challenge.

Purdue Online Writing Lab (OWL)
> https://owl.english.purdue.edu
> Purdue University's Online Writing Lab provides writing resources for students in grades 7–12. Check out their site for tips on coming up with creative writing ideas, starting the writing process, overcoming writer's block, proofreading for errors, and much more.

Scholastic Art and Writing Awards
> http://www.artandwriting.org
> Since 1923 the Scholastic Art and Writing Awards have honored outstanding teen art and writing. Students in grades 7–12 can submit their art or writing for a chance to win scholarships and prizes. Visit the website to learn more.

Stone Soup

http://www.stonesoup.com
Stone Soup magazine publishes writing by kids aged eight through thirteen. Visit the magazine's website to submit your work, read featured stories, and get writing advice from the *Stone Soup* blog. If you're older than thirteen, check out *Teen Ink*.

The Story Starter

http://www.thestorystarter.com
The Story Starter randomly generates more than two hundred billion story-starting sentences such as this one: "The huge turtle trainer dialed the cell phone in the jewelry store at noon for the teacher." Keep clicking until you find a sentence that sparks your fancy, and use part or all of it as a starting point for your own short story.

Strunk, William, Jr., and E. B. White. *The Elements of Style*. New York: Penguin, 2005. First published in 1918, Strunk and White's classic reference book is still a must-have for writers. This slim book is packed with advice about how to write with style. It includes tips about punctuation, grammar, word usage, and how to write clearly and concisely.

Teen Ink

http://www.teenink.com
Teen Ink magazine publishes writing by teens aged thirteen through nineteen. Visit the *Teen Ink* website to submit your work. You can also read the writing of other talented teens and get writing advice in the Writers' Workshop forums.

INDEX